THE NIGHT DRAGONS

DRAGON GIRLS

Phoebe the Moonlight Dragon

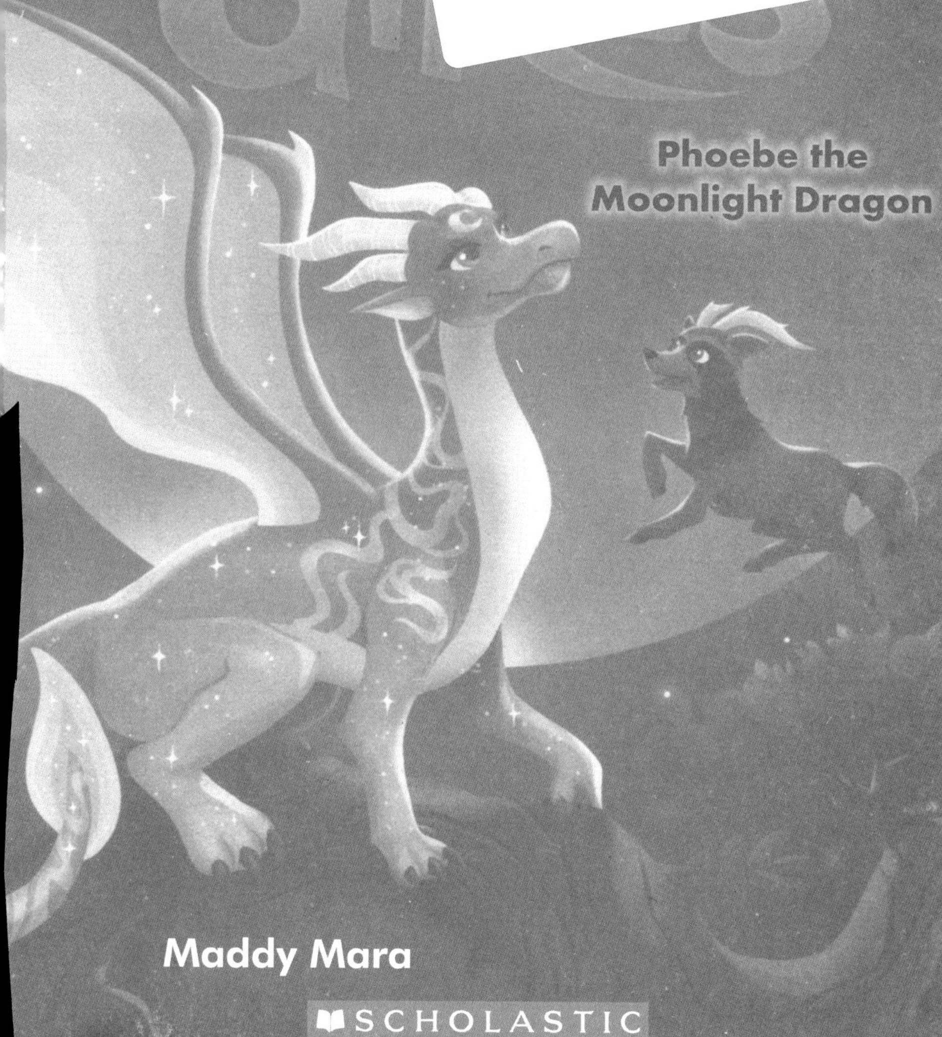

Maddy Mara

SCHOLASTIC

DRAGON GIRLS

Phoebe the Moonlight Dragon

by Maddy Mara

Scholastic Inc.

ISBN 978-93-5471-376-7

First printing 2022
This Reprint edition January 2023
Book design by Cassy Price
Printed in India

The full moon was rising as Phoebe got ready for bed. Tonight it looked closer than usual. The moonlight shone through her window, bathing her room in a beautiful silvery glow that felt magical. Phoebe wasn't a big fan of the dark. In fact, she hated it! But when the moon was big and round like this, it was like having a night-light on. It kept her company and made her feel safe.

Phoebe put her jeans and T-shirt in the laundry basket and slipped into her pajamas. They were her favorite ones, with a swirling galaxy design. Often when she wore them, Phoebe would have dreams about being in a rocket

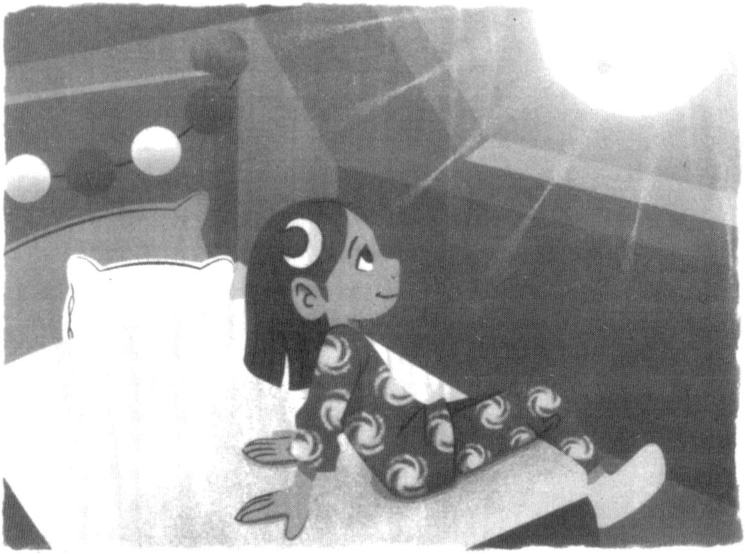

ship, shooting through space. In these dreams, Phoebe was always with her best friends, Rosie and Stella.

The three girls did everything together, including Sleepover Club most Friday nights. The original idea had been that they'd take turns sleeping at one another's houses, but Phoebe often asked Rosie and Stella to sleep at hers. Sometimes she got homesick, especially in the middle of the night when everything was dark and quiet. She felt more relaxed when Sleepover Club was at her home. Then she could make sure that her bedroom door was open just the right amount so that the light from the hallway filtered in. And secretly, she liked knowing her parents were only a couple of rooms away.

At the most recent sleepover, something very strange had happened. Phoebe, Rosie, and Stella had been transported to a magical forest. And in that forest, they had become Dragon Girls! Not just any dragons, either. They were Night Dragons. Their adventure had been like the best dream ever, except it had actually happened.

Phoebe loved feeling so powerful. She often felt nervous in her normal life, but nothing was scary when you were as strong as a dragon. And the flying! It had been a little difficult at first, but the more she practiced, the better she became. Phoebe often dreamed about flying, so actually doing it was incredible. Especially with her friends by her side.

Phoebe pulled on her robe and went to stand by her window. She opened it so the night air flowed in. It had been a warm day, and the evening had yet to cool down completely. Phoebe leaned against her windowsill, looking out over the neighbors' yards.

The Tree Queen, the ruler of the Magic Forest, had told Phoebe and her friends that they would be needed again soon. Phoebe had been worried when she first heard that they were going on a quest. She did not think of herself as brave. But when the Tree Queen explained that the evil Fire Queen was trying to banish nighttime from the Magic Forest, she knew they had to help.

Even though Phoebe didn't like the dark, there were still lots of things she loved about nighttime. Sleepover Club, for instance! Gazing up at the moon each night was wonderful, too, seeing it wax and wane. She also loved snuggling up in her comfy bed and feeling like she was floating on a cloud as she fell asleep. And the way that her dreams took her to all kinds of wild places? That was worth fighting for!

As Phoebe looked up at the moon, she noticed

that the moonlight was different somehow. Rather than its usual pale, silvery color, it was almost aqua.

There was something else strange going on. Phoebe could hear distant singing.

Magic Forest, Magic Forest, come explore . . .

Phoebe felt a tingle of excitement. She had heard that song when she traveled into the Magic Forest last time! That had been on Friday, a Sleepover Club night. But tonight was Tuesday. Was she about to return to the forest anyway? And would Rosie and Stella be there, too?

Phoebe was dying to go back to the Magic Forest, but she knew she wouldn't enjoy it so much if she was alone.

Magic Forest, Magic Forest, come explore . . .

The song was louder now. The aqua light from the moon seemed to be shining directly on Phoebe, bathing her in its cool glow. Phoebe's skin tingled.

Then, Phoebe's bedroom faded as the silvery aqua moonlight washed over her. A gentle breeze picked up, ruffling Phoebe's long dark hair.

Closing her eyes, Phoebe began to sing. She had heard this song only once before, but it was deeply familiar. It was as if she had known it her entire life.

Magic Forest, Magic Forest, come explore.

Magic Forest, Magic Forest, hear my roar!

All of a sudden, the breeze became a fierce wind, encircling Phoebe and lifting her up into the air. Her hair whipped around her as the wind spun her in circles. She breathed in the forest scent of flowers, sweet tropical fruits, and the delicate aroma of magic itself.

Phoebe smiled. Another adventure was about to begin!

When she felt herself touch down to earth, Phoebe cautiously opened her eyes. Was she really back in the Magic Forest? And was she really no longer an ordinary girl, but a fierce dragon?

Looking down, Phoebe saw that her feet had transformed into taloned claws and her legs were covered in shimmering pale blue scales. She certainly looked like a dragon. But just to make sure, she breathed in deeply and let out a loud roar.

Yep, she was definitely a dragon! Phoebe often had vivid dreams, but she'd never had one in which she could roar.

Phoebe looked around in wonder. It was night in the forest, just as it had been at home. But nighttime in the Magic Forest was different from anything Phoebe had ever experienced. The cooling air carried the fresh smell of trees and wilderness. Phoebe was used to city smells, which weren't always nice. And they often seemed stronger at night!

Above the treetops was the deep, velvety blue sky. It looked almost like an ocean. The moon floated near the horizon, looking much bigger than she had ever seen it. The sky in the city never looked as inky and gorgeous as this. The city lights faded it to a dark gray.

Phoebe tilted her face toward the moonlight. She thought the moon had special properties, even though Rosie and Stella teased her that it was just her imagination. Moonlight always made her skin tingle in the best way. With such a big moon, Phoebe was expecting to feel extra tingles tonight. But strangely, her skin felt itchy and irritated, like she was getting sunburned.

"It's a Fire Moon," said a gentle voice in Phoebe's ear.

Hovering in the air beside Phoebe was a very odd, but also very cute, little animal. It looked like an elk, with magnificent antlers reaching up from its head. But this creature had raccoon markings and was smaller than an owl!

"Excuse me, was that you who just spoke?" Phoebe asked.

She knew enough about the Magic Forest to guess that this tiny, flying elk thingy probably *had* spoken to her, but it seemed polite to check.

"Yes," said the little animal. "I'm DasherGirl. And I was just explaining that we have a Fire

Moon. That's why it's so big and its light is sort of prickly. It's also why it is that odd color."

The low-hanging moon definitely had a red tinge to it.

"How often does the Fire Moon come?" asked Phoebe. She had heard of supermoons and blue moons, but never a Fire Moon.

"This is the first in a very, very long time," said DasherGirl. "And it's not a good thing. It's hot rather than cool, and it makes it hard for the creatures of the forest to sleep. That's why the Tree Queen has called on you and the other Night Dragons."

The Fire Moon sounded bad, but Phoebe couldn't help grinning at DasherGirl's words.

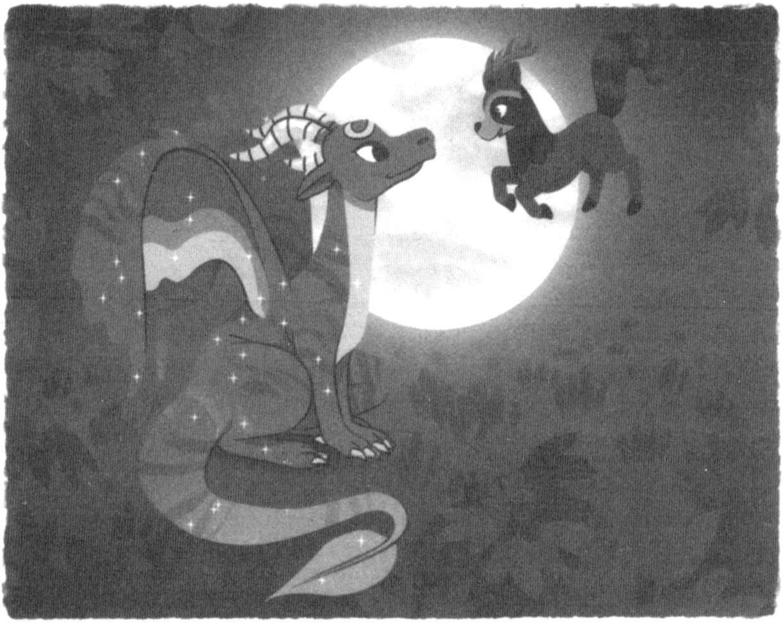

"Rosie and Stella are here?"

"Of course!" said the little elk. "They've just arrived at the Tree Queen's glade. Come on, I'll lead the way. But watch out for Fire Sparks. There are a lot of them around these days."

It was exciting flying through the forest at night. Although it was dark, Phoebe didn't find it hard to see. And her flying skills were getting better and better, so she had no trouble keeping up with DasherGirl as she darted through the trees.

Even though it was the middle of the night, a lot of the forest's daytime animals were active. On the branch of a tree, Phoebe saw a family of squirrels.

"I can't sleep! It's too hot, and my tail feels itchy," she heard a baby squirrel complain.

"My dreams are all wonky!" moaned another little squirrel. "I dreamed I was being chased by a giant acorn."

One of the bigger squirrels pointed up at Phoebe as she flew past. "Look, children. It's a Night Dragon! They'll fix this problem, don't you worry."

Phoebe waved at the family as she flew past, hoping they couldn't tell how nervous their words had made her feel. It seemed like a lot of creatures were depending on her and her friends. She really hoped they didn't let them down!

"Watch out!" DasherGirl called suddenly. "Fire Sparks!"

As Phoebe looked around, she was engulfed in tiny, dazzlingly bright lights. The Fire Sparks buzzed around her eyes and ears, making it impossible to see or hear anything else. They were so terrible! Phoebe usually didn't get very angry, but she could feel annoyance bubbling inside as she twisted and turned to avoid them.

"Stay calm," DasherGirl warned. "Fire Sparks feed off anger and frustration. If you let them get to you, it makes them stronger and brighter. Think about calming things."

It was hard to think about calm things with bright lights buzzing around. It was even harder when you were flying at top speed through a moonlit magic forest!

But Phoebe knew that DasherGirl was right. Breathing in deeply, Phoebe pictured herself

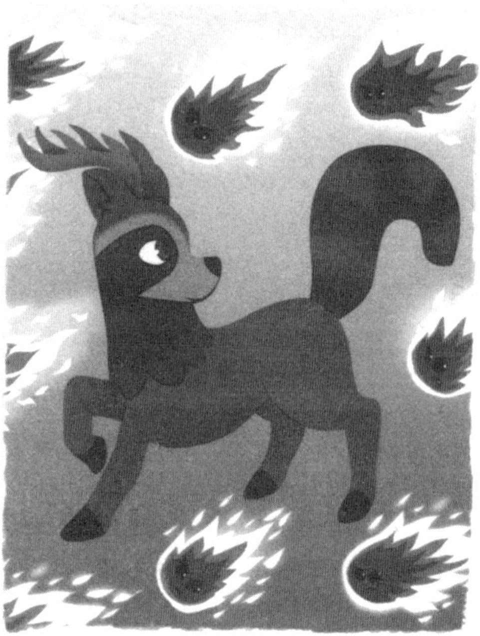

floating on a cloud, bathed in soft moonlight and surrounded by stars.

Instantly, she began to feel better. As she calmed down, she saw the sparks begin to splutter and fade away.

"Great, keep doing whatever you're doing!" DasherGirl cheered.

Phoebe closed her eyes and added to the scene in her mind. She imagined a gentle breeze on her face, and added in soft nighttime sounds. Finally, she put her friends into her dream scene. Having Rosie and Stella nearby always made her feel better.

When she opened her eyes, Phoebe saw the last Fire Spark go out. She grinned to herself. It worked!

DasherGirl did an excited midair loop. "Good work!" she cried. "And perfect timing, because look! We've just arrived at the Tree Queen's glade."

3

Up ahead, Phoebe could see the force field that protected the glade. Inside the shimmering orb, Phoebe could just make out dragonish shapes, moving around. She grinned. Rosie and Stella were already here!

DasherGirl flew up beside her. "I must leave you here," she said, "but we will see each other again soon, I promise." She rubbed her nose against Phoebe's and flew off into the forest.

The light from the Fire Moon spilled across the force field. Was it just Phoebe's imagination, or was the moonlight even redder now? She glanced up. Yes, the moon was definitely a deeper tone. This was bad!

Phoebe took a deep breath and stepped through the force field. It was the best feeling, slipping through the magical air that protected the glade. Inside, the clearing was bathed in a pure silvery moonlight. Here, there were no traces of red at all.

Two magnificent dragons flew over to Phoebe, each wrapping an impressive wing around her.

"Isn't this cool? We're back for another adventure!" said Stella excitedly.

Stella was deep purple and yellow. She was the Starlight Dragon, and was covered in stars.

Phoebe nodded. "It's really exciting," she agreed. "Have you heard what our quest is this time?"

"Not yet," said Rosie. She was the Twilight Dragon, and her scales were pink and purple. "The queen is still in her tree form."

As Rosie spoke, the glade filled with the sound

of rustling leaves. The Night Dragons turned to look at the elegant tree in the center of the glade. It swayed back and forth, almost like it was dancing. The swaying became stronger until the trunk of the tree had transformed into a regal-looking tree woman. She had long, flowing hair and wore an elegant moss-green gown.

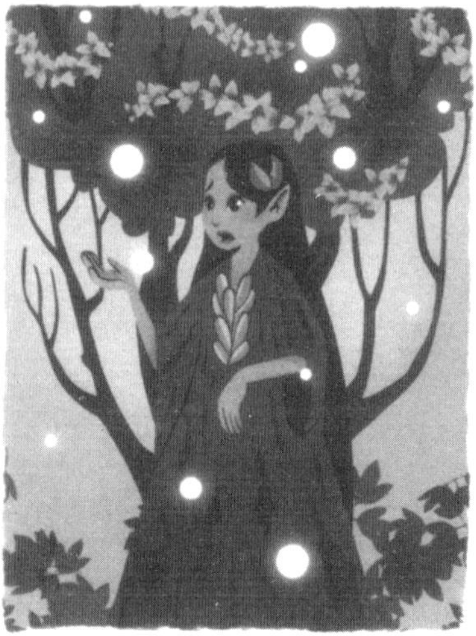

Two of the tree's branches had become long arms, which the Tree Queen now spread out in a welcoming gesture.

"Hello, my Night Dragons!" she said in her strong, warm voice. "It is so good to have you back. Your help is greatly needed, as I am sure you have already noticed."

"Yes, there's a Fire Moon!" Phoebe exclaimed. "And it's messing up everyone's sleep. It's because of the Fire Queen and her sparks."

She usually felt nervous talking to people she didn't know very well, especially grown-ups. But somehow the Tree Queen was different.

"Exactly, Phoebe," said the Tree Queen.

"Nighttime is extremely important here in the Magic Forest. It's when the Dreamlets hatch."

"Dreamlets?" repeated Rosie, looking curious. "What are they?"

One of the things Phoebe loved about her friend Rosie was how she often asked the very question that was on Phoebe's lips!

"They are young dreams," explained the Tree Queen. "Every night, a new batch of Dreamlets is born. They move throughout the forest, finding sleeping creatures they can whisper their stories to. The stories turn into dreams. And dreams are very important! They help us sort through the problems of the day and learn new things. It's how birds improve their flying, for example. Or how rabbits learn to leap farther than they ever have."

Phoebe nodded. She got it. Sometimes, during the day, Phoebe felt scared of trying new things. But in her dreams, she could do anything. After she had managed to do something in her sleep, she sometimes felt brave enough to try it in real life.

Like with handstands, which Phoebe had never been any good at doing. Then one night, she had dreamed about doing handstands. When she woke up, the first thing she did was try one out. Right there in her bedroom, for the first time ever, Phoebe had done a perfect handstand!

"Recently, there have been fewer Dreamlets in the forest," continued the Tree Queen. "We do not know what the problem is. But I have heard there is something going wrong in the hatchery."

"Hatchery?" Rosie asked.

"Where the Dreamlets are nursed," explained the Tree Queen. "Once they're strong enough, they can leave the hatchery and spread their vital dreams."

"So you'd like us to go and check out what's happening there?" Stella guessed.

The Tree Queen's leaves rustled as she nodded. "The hatchery is near the Moon Lake. You will recognize it when you see it. Phoebe, I'd like you to lead this quest."

Phoebe was too surprised to say anything. She wasn't really the leading type. She didn't know if she wanted to lead a quest. What if she messed up?

But the Tree Queen looked at her with a kind smile. "You will be a wonderful leader, Phoebe," she said gently. "Here, this is for you."

She held out something glittery to Phoebe. It was a ball of magic thread on a chain. It didn't look like much, but it had come in very handy when Phoebe and her friends were on their last quest.

Phoebe stepped forward and bowed her head so the queen could slip the delicate chain around her neck.

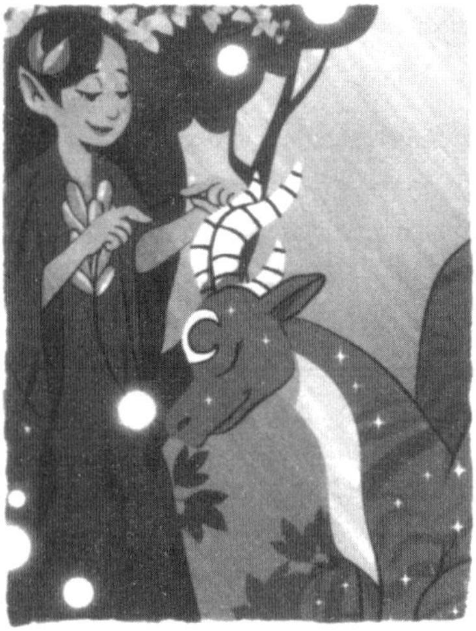

Looking down at it, she felt a surge of pride. Against her scales, the necklace twinkled. *I can do this*, she told herself. *And it's not like I will be alone. I'll have Rosie and Stella with me.*

Stella gave her a friendly nudge. "What do you think, boss?" she asked teasingly. "Should we get going?"

Phoebe nodded. The sooner they figured out

what was going on, the better. That Fire Moon made her feel uneasy.

"Night Dragons," said the Tree Queen, swishing her branches. "One last thing before you go. The Fire Moon creates irritation and bad feelings in those touched by its light. But anger gives the Fire Queen and her Fire Sparks more power. They feed off discontent. You must be very careful."

Phoebe had noticed this. "We will," she promised the Tree Queen.

The three Night Dragons took off into the Magic Forest.

The Fire Moon cast a strange glow over the trees and made Phoebe's stomach tighten with worry. Clearly, there was no time to waste.

"Which way should we go?" Stella called as they flew higher.

"The Tree Queen said we should head to the Moon Lake. That could be anywhere!" Phoebe sighed as she scanned the treetops. She felt like she was already doing badly, and the quest hadn't even begun.

"Hey, Phoebe," Rosie said, swooping closer, glinting pink and purple in the moonlight. "The thread you're wearing around your neck might help. It helped me."

As Rosie spoke, Phoebe felt the chain give a gentle tug. The end of the thread unwound itself just a little and stretched out. It was pointing which way to go!

"Follow me!" Phoebe called, zooming to the front of the trio.

The Night Dragons flew over the vast forest. The treetops below them swayed gently in the moonlight. Every now and then, a birdcall or animal cry floated up, reminding Phoebe that there were a lot of creatures depending on her and her friends.

The thread kept tugging her gently in one direction until suddenly it stopped pointing ahead and started pointing down instead. Phoebe glanced below her and gasped. There glimmered a vast lake, perfectly round and so still it looked like a mirror. Reflected in the lake's center was the moon, like a huge, shimmering pearl inside its shell.

"That *has* to be the Moon Lake, right?" called Stella.

Phoebe felt the thread tug downward again. She nodded. "Definitely," she said.

The three friends whooshed down through the dark air and landed near the lake. All around it, steep, rocky cliffs rose up toward the sky.

"I wonder where the Dreamlet hatchery is?" Rosie asked.

Just then, the sandy soil around them began to move. Soon, hundreds of tiny lizard-like creatures began popping up through the sand. Each of the creatures glowed as if lit by a neon light. A purple egg balanced on each animal's back.

The creatures stared at the Night Dragons with amazed expressions on their tiny faces.

"You are the biggest Newt Nurses I've ever seen!" one declared with a flick of its bright blue tongue. "And where are your eggs?"

"I hope you haven't lost them," said another. "That's all we need right now."

"We're not Newt Nurses," Phoebe said. "We're Night Dragons. We've been sent by the Tree Queen to help. She says there's been trouble here in the hatchery?"

More newts, each with an egg carefully

balanced on its back, padded over on their surprisingly big feet.

"It's true!" one cried. "It's the Fire Moon. The Dreamlet eggs will only hatch when the conditions are just right. This moon is far too hot!"

Phoebe exhaled, thinking hard. As her breath left her nostrils, it formed a pale cloud, shining like moonlight. The cloud hovered in the air, then sank down toward one of the eggs resting on the back of a newt.

When it touched the egg, the cloud melted over it, covering it in a soft blue haze.

"Look! The egg is hatching!" squeaked one of the newts. "Your roar must have cooled it to the perfect temperature."

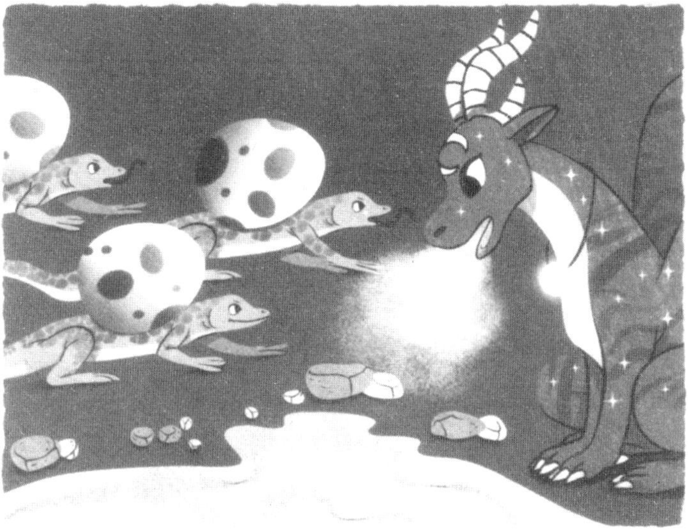

The egg began to shiver and shake. There was a loud *CRACK!* The top part of the shell shattered and fell to the ground.

Phoebe watched it closely. What was going to come out? As she stared, a tiny, soft, worm-like creature peered out and looked around. It had large blue eyes and stripy pink-and-purple fur.

"Who would have thought that a worm could be so cute!" Stella said, clasping her paws.

"I'm not a worm!" the Dreamlet said in a sweet singsong voice. "Can worms do this?"

The little animal wiggled up to the edge of its shell and then, to everyone's surprise, launched itself into the air!

"Catch it!" Rosie cried in alarm. "It'll fall!"

But there was no need to worry. The Dreamlet did not fall. Instead, it began to wriggle through the air just like a normal worm does on land.

Phoebe turned to her friends. "Maybe if we roar together, we can cool down all the eggs and help them hatch?" she suggested.

She knew it sounded like a very strange

suggestion. Surely a dragon's roar would be hot? They definitely didn't want scrambled eggs. But it seemed like a Night Dragon's roar might be the opposite. Powerful, but cooling.

"Fantastic idea!" said Stella as Rosie nodded enthusiastically.

"Okay, then," said Phoebe, filling her chest with air. "One, two, THREE!"

Together, Phoebe, Rosie, and Stella roared as loudly as they could. A huge plume of smoke—purple and pink and blue and even a touch of yellow—swirled in the air above the hatchery. Then, slowly but surely, the smoke from their roars began to lower.

The Newt Nurses all scurried around,

arranging themselves so that they were below the cloud. Phoebe held her breath. Was this going to work?

The roar cloud finally settled over the eggs, changing them from a shiny white to a pale blue.

And then the eggs began to hatch! Phoebe decided it was a bit like waiting for corn to pop. At first one cracked, then another. But before long, the eggs were all cracking at once, in all directions!

As the top of each egg opened, a little Dreamlet wiggled out. Soon the air above the Moon Lake was filled with little ribbons of wriggling pinks and purples.

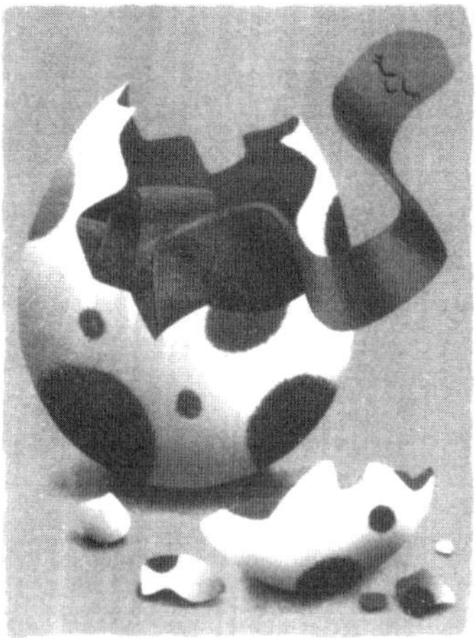

Suddenly, the newts began to stamp their large feet on the ground. Phoebe turned to her friends, eyebrows up. Were the newts upset about something? But they were smiling! This must be their way of clapping.

"You did it, Night Dragons!" one of them called. "You saved—"

The newt was cut short by a sudden flash of light. It was so blinding that for a moment

Phoebe couldn't see a thing. She blinked several times to clear the red light from her eyes.

"What *was* that?" Stella asked, rubbing her eyes with her paws.

Before anyone could answer, a cry went up from the Newt Nurses. "The babies! They're GONE!"

A moment ago, the air had been full of adorable and wriggly little Dreamlets. Now there was nothing there at all.

"That bright flash must have been the Fire Sparks," Phoebe said.

Stella nodded. "We have to find them! They can't have gotten far."

Rosie agreed. "But which direction did they go? I didn't see a thing!"

Phoebe scanned the area. Where had the

Fire Sparks taken them? Even with her powerful eyesight, Phoebe couldn't see any sign of the Dreamlets. It was as though they'd disappeared into thin air.

Suddenly, out of the corner of her eye, Phoebe spotted something moving near where the cliffs met the lake. She flapped her wings and leapt over toward the spot.

There, snagged in the long grass, was a single pink-and-purple Dreamlet.

Phoebe untangled the wriggly little thing and held it carefully in her paw. Stella and Rosie bounded over to her side, followed by a swarm of very anxious Newt Nurses.

"If we have no Dreamlets, then none of the

forest creatures will be able to dream," one of the Newt Nurses muttered to the others. "And if they can't dream, they will start to get sick."

Phoebe raised the Dreamlet to her face. She felt huge compared with the tiny creature, so she tried to speak very softly.

"Where did the others go?" she asked gently.

The Dreamlet gazed at Phoebe for a moment. Then it leapt from her paw and into the air. It began wriggling over to the cliff face.

"Is it trying to escape? Maybe it's scared of us?" Rosie said.

Phoebe shook her head. "I think it's trying to show us something. Look!" Phoebe pointed to a hole in the rock face near where the Dreamlet was wriggling. It looked like the mouth of a cave.

Phoebe flew over and peered inside. It was very deep and very dark. Then she saw something that made her gasp. "Something is glowing down there! It HAS to be the Fire Sparks!" she shouted to the others. Stella and Rosie flew to join her.

Phoebe would never normally climb into a deep, dark hole without knowing what was down there. She was not that sort of dare-devil. But being a Night Dragon made her feel so capable, especially when she had Stella and Rosie with her.

"Be careful!" called the newts. "The ground

below this place is ancient and holds all kinds of powerful magic. Strange things happen down there. Watch out."

Phoebe felt a shiver travel up her long, curved spine. But this did not change her mind. She turned to her friends.

"Ready?" she asked.

Stella and Rosie answered in one voice. "Let's go!"

Phoebe tucked her wings around her torso and squeezed through the gap. It was dark, but once inside, she could see that the cave was wide enough for her to fly. She spread her wings and began to soar down the passage. Luckily, she could hear Rosie and Stella just behind her. That stopped her from feeling afraid.

They flew along a tunnel that sloped downward. The occasional tree root broke through the rocky sides, and sometimes a drip of water fell on Phoebe's wings as they beat in the dank underground air.

We're directly below the Moon Lake! Phoebe realized.

As Phoebe turned a bend, the tunnel widened and she found herself in a huge open space. She landed softly, and her friends did the same. Phoebe could hear rushing water but could not quite make out where the sound was coming from.

She gave a quick roar. The glowing light from

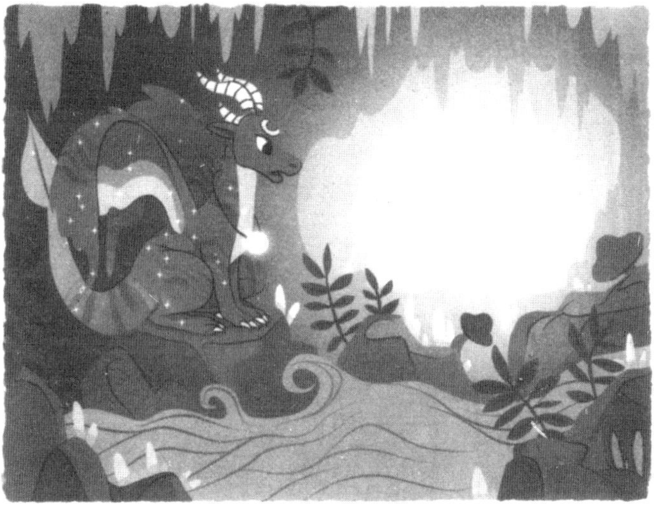

her roar spread out, illuminating the space in beautiful cool blues.

What Phoebe saw made her gasp. They were in an underground garden, filled with the strangest flowers and plants she had ever seen. It was both creepy and beautiful. *These must be night plants*, thought Phoebe, *ones that thrive away from the light.*

Most surprising of all was the river flowing through the garden. This was clearly no ordinary river. The water was a mass of different colors. Shade of purple, blue, orange, green, and pink twisted and twirled around one another as the water rushed along.

"Look!" Stella shouted.

There, on the other side of the river, were the Dreamlets! When they spotted the Night Dragons, the creatures whizzed around in big, happy loops.

But Phoebe noticed something strange. Every time a Dreamlet flew to the river's edge, they would leap back as though something had stung them.

"I wonder why they don't just fly over to us?" Rosie mused.

"Maybe they're scared?" Stella suggested.

Phoebe heard a familiar voice in her ear. DasherGirl was back! "They can't fly across," she said, settling by Phoebe's side. "There is an electrical current reaching from the surface of the water all the way to the roof of the cave. It forms an invisible barrier. It's impossible to cross the river unless you are surrounded by Fire Sparks. They are the only creatures in the forest who can get through."

Phoebe frowned. This was so annoying. They had come so far! The Fire Sparks were always trying to get the better of them. It was starting to make Phoebe feel angry, even though it usually took a lot to upset her.

She took a deep breath, remembering that the Tree Queen had warned them that feeling grumpy only fed the Fire Sparks. "Is there any way over there?" she asked DasherGirl.

"Yes, but you won't like it. The only way is underwater," explained the elk, shaking her antlers in a way that made it clear she did not like this option, either.

Phoebe looked at the surging river. She knew how to swim as a *normal* girl. But what was it like swimming as a *Dragon* Girl? And in water like this?

“You and the other Night Dragons will be strong enough to swim through the current,” said DasherGirl. “But this is the Dream River. Its water can send you to sleep. Once you are in the water, you must swim as fast as you can to the other side. And you must try not to get any water in your eyes or mouth.”

Phoebe looked at the Dreamlets, wriggling in the air on the other side of the Dream River. She turned to DasherGirl.

“What happens if you get the water in your eyes or mouth?” she asked, not sure if she wanted to hear the answer.

“The dreams might be too strong,” DasherGirl

explained softly. "They could overpower you."

Phoebe was used to having vivid dreams. Crossing was going to be dangerous. But if anyone could do it, it was Phoebe the Moonlight Dragon.

Slowly, Phoebe slipped into the surging river, with DasherGirl riding on her shoulder. Phoebe took a deep breath and began to swim. The water felt surprisingly warm. Even though the current was strong, Phoebe found that it wasn't too difficult to swim across. The tricky part was making sure none of the water got into her eyes or mouth.

She heard a splash as her friends jumped into the water behind her.

"Am I imagining it, or is the river getting wider?" Stella asked, swimming up alongside Phoebe.

It didn't make sense, but the river looked much bigger now that they were in it.

"It's got such a sweet smell," Rosie commented. "It reminds me of Dad's hot chocolate before bed." She yawned. "It's making me sleepy, actually."

"Don't fall asleep!" called Phoebe, remembering DasherGirl's warning. "Come on, let's get to the other side as quickly as possible."

But they had swum only a few more strokes when flickering orange-and-yellow shapes rose up out of the water. DasherGirl shook her hooves in panic.

"The river is on fire!" Stella gasped. "Do we turn back?"

"Wait," said Phoebe. She slowly moved closer to the flames, noticing that the water did not get hotter as she did so. "They're not real flames," she called to her friends. "I think they're like a dream. One we can all see."

When she said this, the flames disappeared.

The Night Dragons continued to swim, but Phoebe could feel her heart pounding.

DasherGirl quivered by her ear. Phoebe wasn't surprised. This was scary!

The water in front of her began to bubble. Slowly, slowly, the head of a huge alligator emerged out of the water. The alligator had fiery eyes. When it opened its mouth, Phoebe saw two rows of gleaming sharp teeth.

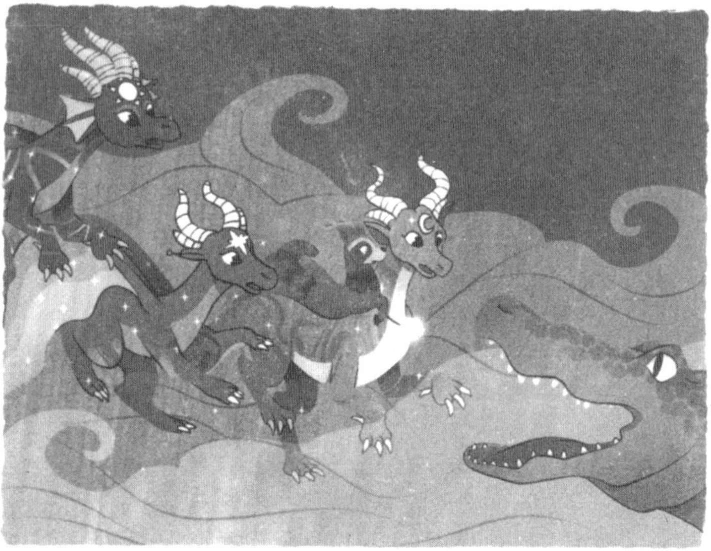

"It's just another dream," Phoebe yelled out, even though her voice cracked with fear. "A bad one. Just ignore it and keep going."

The alligator was not happy to be called a dream. It reared up one last time, snapping at the air with its powerful jaws as it sank back down into the water and disappeared.

"Well done!" cooed DasherGirl.

The other bank was close now, but the sweet chocolate scent of the river was getting stronger. The smell made it so hard for Phoebe to keep her eyes open. Maybe she could shut them just for a moment?

Turning to look behind her, Phoebe saw that her friends were struggling, too. Seeing their drooping eyelids helped wake her up.

"We're almost there!" she called to Rosie and Stella.

As she spoke, the water began to churn again. Phoebe's stomach dropped. Another dream was surely coming. What would it be this time? She wondered what could be scarier than a fire or an enormous alligator.

She was surprised when a huge bed rose up out of the river. *What was scary about a soft, puffy bed?*

"Oh, that looks so comfy," Stella sighed.

A fluffy sheep jumped out of the water on one side of the bed. It soared through the air, bleating, and splashed back down into the river. A moment later another sheep made the same leap. Then another.

"One sheep, two sheep, three sheep," counted Rosie as she swam. She yawned even more loudly. "I'll never understand why counting sheep makes me so sleepy."

When even DasherGirl started yawning, Phoebe understood why this dream was the scariest of all. If they fell asleep in the river, it would be extremely dangerous.

Phoebe racked her brain. There must be something she could do. She grinned as an idea came to her.

She began to sing at the top of her voice. And she sang not only very loudly, but as badly as she could, too.

Don't count SHEEEEEP!

Don't go to SLEEEEEEP!

"Ow! That hurts my ears!" Stella grumbled.

"Mine, too," said Rosie. "What are you *doing*?"

"I'm singing an anti-lullaby!" Phoebe yelled back. "This is not time for snoozing. It's time for SWIMMING! Sing with me, you two."

Rosie, Stella, and even DasherGirl joined Phoebe in singing—loudly and badly—until they finally reached the far side of the river. The

Night Dragons pulled themselves up onto the riverbank and lay there for a moment, breathing deeply and recovering from the difficult swim.

The Dreamlets wriggled along the ground toward them, making funny little peeping noises and butting their tiny heads against one another.

"They're not flying anymore," Rosie observed. "I wonder why."

Phoebe sat up and looked at the Dreamlets. As she watched, a few tried to leap into the air. But now none of them could get higher than an inch or two before they fell back down to the ground.

"They're too weak," she said.

DasherGirl nodded. "Dreamlets need the moonlight after they've been hatched. Otherwise they lose the strength to fly."

Phoebe stood up. "We'd better get them back across the river."

Stella shook her head. "We need a break," she said. "A few minutes won't make any difference. I'm exhausted."

Phoebe felt frustration flare inside her. The Dreamlets needed them. "We don't *have* a few minutes, Stella!" Phoebe snapped.

Stella frowned. "No need to be like that," she said.

"Hey! Stop it, you two," said Rosie.

Phoebe knew she shouldn't have snapped. And she knew that Rosie just trying to help. But somehow that made everything worse. Her whole body buzzed with irritation.

DasherGirl flew up to her ear. "Remember, the Fire Sparks feed off anger!" she warned.

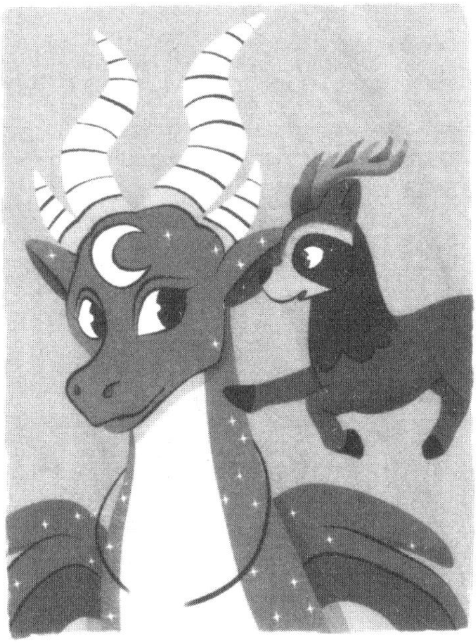

Phoebe's heart sank as she remembered what the Tree Queen had said. She could already see tiny sparks of fire flittering in the darkness, heading their way.

Before she dealt with the Fire Sparks, Phoebe had something just as important to do. She took a deep breath and turned to her friend. "Stella, I'm sorry. I don't know what got into me." Instantly, everything seemed better.

"I do; it's those Fire Sparks," Stella said kindly. "I'm sorry, too."

For the millionth time, Phoebe thanked her lucky stars she had such good friends.

Now, what to do? There was no time to swim back across the river. Phoebe squeezed her eyes shut. There *had* to be a solution. She just needed to figure out what it was!

Phoebe felt something tug at her neck. When she opened her eyes, she saw that the bundle of magic thread had begun to unravel and was pointing up toward the roof of the cave.

DasherGirl began to fly in excited circles. "Of course! That thread is partly made from moonlight. It will always find the quickest way back to moonlight."

"There must be a gap in the rocks!" Phoebe cried.

They scanned the rocks above them. Thanks to their powerful eyesight, the Night Dragons could see the roof of the cave quite clearly. Sure enough, there was a large crack up there.

Phoebe had an idea. She grabbed hold of a section of magic thread, and with all her dragon strength, she flung it up high like a lasso. It soared through the air and disappeared through the gap.

"Great throw," Rosie said as a deep, groaning sound came from the roof.

Small rocks and dirt began to tumble down.

"Protect the Dreamlets!" Phoebe cried.

The Night Dragons spread their wings across the little creatures.

"It's like an umbrella made of dragon wings!" Stella chuckled.

Soon the rocks stopped falling. The Night Dragons lowered their wings and looked up. The crack in the rocks above was wider than before. Weirdly, the thread was also thicker and sturdier than it had been originally. It now looked more like rope.

Even better, it had begun to glow like pure silver.

"It's found a pathway to the moonlight!"

DasherGirl said, waving her tail.

Phoebe thought she could probably squeeze though the gap in the rocks now, but it wasn't wide enough for flying.

DasherGirl seemed to know what she was thinking. "You will have to climb up," she explained. "As the Moonlight Dragon, you'll be fine."

"And Rosie and Stella will be, too, right?" Phoebe said.

DasherGirl shook her head. "Moonbeam ropes are difficult to climb. You are the only Night Dragon with moonlight flowing through your veins."

Phoebe hated the idea of leaving her friends

down here. Plus, she didn't want to take the Dreamlets up a rope all by herself.

"Why don't you try at least?" she urged Stella and Rosie.

First Rosie and then Stella took turns tugging on the moonbeam rope. But both were able to climb only a short way before they slipped back down to the ground.

"It's impossible to hold on to!" Stella groaned.

Rosie agreed. "It's so slippery! And I'm still pooped from that swim." This was not what Phoebe wanted to hear.

A few Fire Sparks appeared and buzzed around Phoebe. They seemed to know when she was getting frustrated almost before she did. Phoebe took a deep, calming breath. Then she nodded and smiled. She felt her angry feelings flitter away until she felt like her normal, calm self again.

"Okay, you rest here. I'll take the Dreamlets up. Then we'll figure out a way to get you out." She turned to the Dreamlets. "You guys, climb onto my back," she instructed them. "And don't let go."

In a flash, the Dreamlets wriggled up onto Phoebe's back, tail, and head. They were very warm and a little ticklish.

"You kind of look like cotton candy," chuckled Stella. "Cotton candy with a dragon tail."

"Nah," Rosie said, tilting her head to get a

better look. "You look more like a fancy feather duster."

Despite the situation, Phoebe couldn't help laughing. Her friends knew how to make her feel good, no matter how serious things were.

Laughing also cleared away the remains of her negative feelings, and Phoebe grabbed hold of the magic rope, ready to climb.

As soon as she touched the moonbeam rope, it was clear DasherGirl had been right. Phoebe could feel the power of the moon surging through her.

"You're glowing like a full moon!" Rosie marveled.

Phoebe expected the climbing to be difficult,

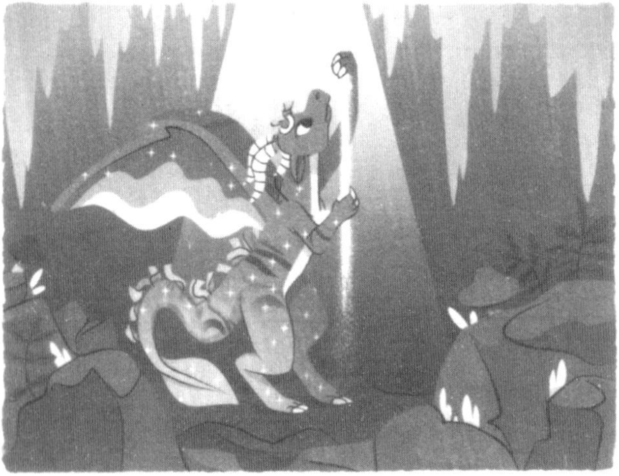

especially after seeing her friends struggle. But for Phoebe, the climb was easy. In fact, it almost felt like the moon-charged rope was pulling her up.

Phoebe climbed quickly and smoothly. Up and up she went. Soon she reached the gap in the rocks. As she climbed through, her way was lit up by the glow of the rope and her own scales.

At this point, the Dreamlets began to hum a happy little tune.

Nearly there! thought Phoebe.

Right near the top, the gap in the rocks narrowed. Phoebe wasn't sure if she was going to fit through.

"Hold tight!" she warned the Dreamlets. "This is going to be squishy."

Clutching on to the moonbeam rope, Phoebe reached one strong claw up after the other. She could finally see the moon above her, beaming down. It was looking redder than ever, which was a worry. Still, she'd nearly made it back to the surface.

But as she edged through the narrow gap

with the Dreamlets clinging to her back, Phoebe felt a sharp pain in her leg. *Ouch!* She looked down and saw a pointy rock jutting out. There was a deep cut in her scales, and it oozed blood. But this was not ordinary red blood. This was a pale silvery color. It was like pure moonlight. DasherGirl was right. She really did have moonlight running through her veins!

Phoebe gritted her teeth as the wound began to throb. She couldn't let this accident stop her. Gripping hard on the rope, she tried to keep climbing. Pain tore up her leg. It was no good. The cut was too deep.

This can't be happening! Phoebe groaned to

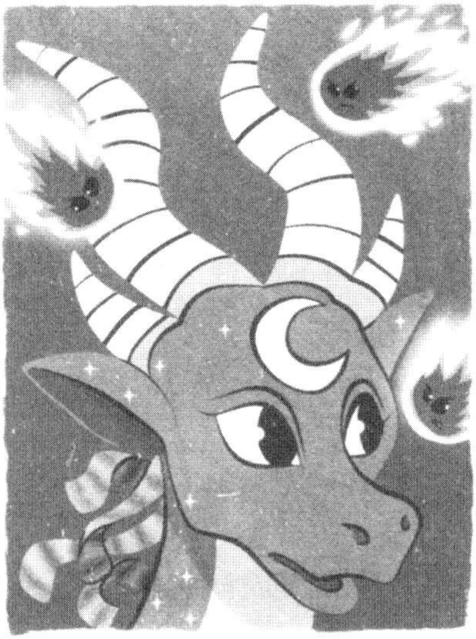

herself. It was so annoying to be so close that she could feel the moonlight on her face but not be able to make it out. How was she going to climb when she couldn't move her leg?

There was a crackling sound, and a cluster of blazing Fire Sparks appeared. It was bad enough dealing with the Fire Sparks when she could swish them away with her wings and powerful tail. It was much worse when she was climbing a rope with a badly injured leg!

The Dreamlets on Phoebe's back had stopped their happy singing and were making little worried sounds. The more frustrated Phoebe became, the more Fire Sparks appeared. Soon they were buzzing all around her face, like flies in a scorching desert. Worse, they were frightening the Dreamlets.

This was *not* how she wanted this quest to go.

The ground began to shudder. Phoebe looked around. Was that an earthquake? But then she noticed a glowing blue-and-purple mist. She watched as the mist gathered around her bleeding leg. Strangely, the throbbing seemed to fade a bit. As the mist settled, it also looked like the bleeding was slowing down.

A huge grin stretched across Phoebe's dragon face. This was no earthquake. This was the roar of her friends!

"That's so smart!" DasherGirl said, shaking her antlers in delight. "They're roaring, and because they're such good friends, their roar is healing you!"

The Dreamlets let out a happy cheer. If they'd had hands, Phoebe was pretty sure they'd be clapping them.

Phoebe tried to wriggle her foot. Her leg still hurt, but it was better than it had been a few moments ago.

Maybe it will help if I roar, too? she wondered.

It was worth a try. She filled her lungs and

roared. It billowed up, illuminating everything in a moonlight-colored fog. A moment later, she heard her friends joining in.

The Dreamlets tried to roar as well. It was more like squealing than roaring, but Phoebe appreciated the effort.

Phoebe watched in delight as the roar gathered like a healing bandage around her wound. The throbbing stopped, and when the mist cleared, Phoebe gasped. Not only had the bleeding stopped, but the gash had disappeared entirely!

Even better, the power of their roar caused the rocks all around her to crumble. Dust swirled, joining the glow of the Night Dragons' roars. With a loud groan, the earth seemed to split open.

The Dreamlets squealed in delight. There was now enough space for Phoebe to stretch out her wings.

"Hold on, Dreamlets," she called. "It's time to fly!"

Phoebe flapped her wings and flew up the last little way to the surface. It was wonderful to land on the soft grass and feel the night air against her scales.

The Dreamlets jumped off her back and quickly wriggled over to a patch of moonlight.

Phoebe watched as the magical rope shrank

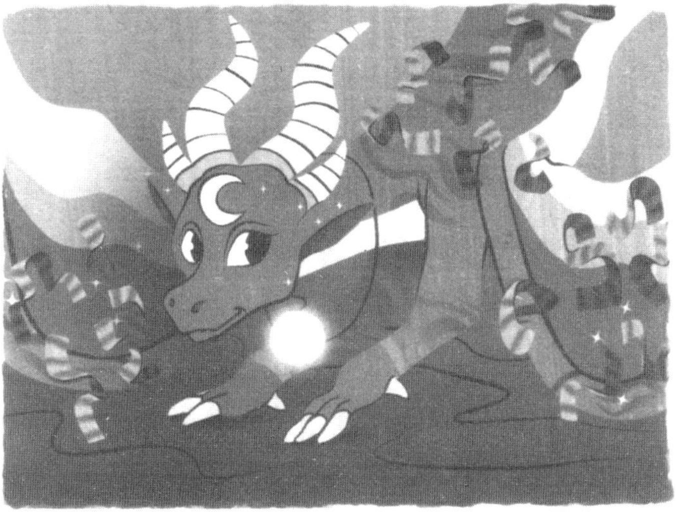

to its normal size and floated back to join the ball of thread suspended from her necklace. Up in the sky, the Fire Moon was living up to its name. It looked like it could catch the sky on fire.

She hoped the moonlight would be cool enough to recharge the Dreamlets, even if it was fiery moonlight. There was something else on her mind, too. Her friends! How was she going to get them out of the underground cave? They had helped her get out of a tight spot. Now it was her turn to help them.

But happily, this was one thing Phoebe did not have to worry about. Stella and Rosie burst out of the hole and flopped onto the grass beside her, breathless but laughing.

"So it turns out that I am not very good at flying straight up!" Stella said, rubbing her head with her wing.

"Yeah, I figured that by the way you kept headbutting my tail!" Rosie chuckled.

Phoebe was SO happy to see them! All the

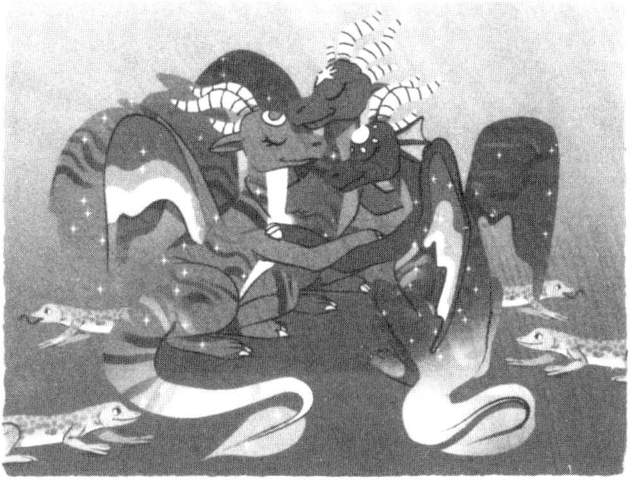

tension she had felt down in the cave had disappeared, and the three friends hugged.

"That was amazing," Phoebe said, shaking her head in disbelief. "How did you know that your roar would heal my leg?"

"We didn't! We just wanted to roar our support," Rosie said.

"There's not much our roars can't do," Stella

said proudly. "Hey, look who's here!" She pulled out of the hug.

Behind them, the Newt Nurses had appeared and were busy fussing over the Dreamlets.

"Are they okay?" Phoebe called.

"They're not hurt," reported one of the nearby newts, "but they are weak. The Fire Moon is not giving them the nourishment they need. They need to get closer to the moon. Can you take them to the Dream Clouds?"

Phoebe and her friends looked at one another. On their last quest they had gone to the Hope Clouds. Were the Dream Clouds similar?

As usual, DasherGirl seemed to know what the Night Dragons were thinking. "The Dream

Clouds are a layer higher than the Hope Clouds," she explained.

"Do we go back to the sunset ray station?" Rosie asked. "Or can we fly?"

DasherGirl shook her little head. "You can't fly that high. And the moon is up, so the sunset rays have set. You will have to use a moonbeam spring to get up there."

Phoebe wasn't sure she liked the sound of a moonbeam spring. In the real world she was NOT into wild activities like bungee jumping. It was the sort of thing she watched online and thought, *I'll never, ever do that!*

But Phoebe was learning that she was capable of far more than she'd realized in the Magic

Forest. If DasherGirl thought it was possible to spring through the air on a moonbeam, then maybe it was! There did seem to be an obvious problem, though.

"Where do we get a moonbeam?" she asked. "It's not like they're just lying around."

The Newt Nurses all looked at her in surprise. "There's one right there!" The nearest newt pointed.

Sure enough, a beam of moonlight was shining through the clouds and hitting the edge of the Moon Lake. It glowed with silvery magic. Phoebe reached out her paw, expecting it to pass through the milky blue light.

Instead, her paw felt the moonbeam as a solid, tingling rope.

"That's it!" said DasherGirl. "Moonbeams are stronger and bouncier than anything else in the Magic Forest."

Phoebe gave her moonbeam a little pull and felt it bounce back up with a force that flung her into the air. She shouted with joy as she landed back on the ground.

"Guys," she called. "This is SO fun. You pull the moonbeam down and it catapults you into the sky!"

Rosie and Stella quickly found glowing moonbeams of their own to test.

Once they were all set, the Newt Nurses bustled around getting the Dreamlets arranged on the backs of the dragons.

"Behave yourselves, little ones," the Newt Nurses told their small charges. "And make sure you soak up as much moonlight as you can on the Dream Clouds. It will make you big and strong."

The Dreamlets made soft, sleepy sounds by way of reply.

Phoebe smiled at her friends.

"Ready?" she asked.

"Ready," called Stella and Rosie.

Gripping tightly onto her moonbeam, Phoebe

took a breath, tucked in her wings, and pulled with all her might. The powerful moonbeam sprang back with incredible force.

Phoebe was zooming toward the clouds!

The air rushed past Phoebe's scales as she and the others whooshed up through the night sky. Higher and higher they soared. Soon the clouds loomed large up ahead.

"This is amazing!" Stella whooped. She was soaring along, holding tight to her moonbeam and smiling from one dragon ear to the other.

Not far behind was Rosie, who had wrapped the moonbeam around her middle and was doing twirls like a circus performer.

DasherGirl fluttered beside Phoebe. "The Dream Clouds are just ahead," she reported.

Phoebe could see a thick layer of silvery cloud. It looked like it had been sprinkled with glitter.

"Once we pass into the clouds, let go of your moonbeam," DasherGirl said. "I'll tell you when."

Phoebe closed her eyes as they entered the silvery clouds. She got a whiff of lavender. When she opened her eyes again, Phoebe and her friends were on the other side of the clouds.

"Okay, Night Dragons. Let go of your moonbeams now!" instructed DasherGirl.

Phoebe took a deep breath and let go. She and the others stopped zooming up, and for a moment were suspended in midair. Then they floated down toward the layer of clouds just below. The clouds were puffy and beautiful except for the reddish glow cast on them by the Fire Moon.

"We can't fly up here, right?" asked Stella as they drifted lower.

"No, but look! We can use our wings to glide." Rosie stretched out her elegant twilight-colored wings.

Phoebe and Stella did the same, and together, the three friends landed on the huge Dream Cloud.

They were suddenly surrounded by little cloudlike creatures.

"Are they Sky Skimmers?" Stella whispered. "They look a bit like the ones we met on our last quest."

"Hmm, these are different. They're more wispy and see-through," Rosie said.

"We are cousins," one of the little cloud creatures explained. "But there's no time to chat about family resemblances. What has happened to these Dreamlets?"

"They are so thin and weak," cried another

Sky Skimmer, sounding outraged. "Who has been looking after them?"

Phoebe knew that the Sky Skimmers did not mean to be rude. But the Dragon Girls had been through so much to get the Dreamlets here. A thank-you would be nice!

Suddenly, a gasp went up among the Sky Skimmers. "NOOOO! How did THEY get here?"

Phoebe's insides lurched. Fire Sparks! The Sky Skimmers whooshed back and forth in a panic.

"Fire Sparks have NEVER been this high before!" DasherGirl said. "The Dream Clouds have always been a safe space for the dreams of the forest. This is very serious!"

As DasherGirl was speaking, Phoebe smelled something. Something awful. Whirling around, she saw that wherever the Fire Sparks were buzzing, the clouds were smoking! Would they catch fire? The angry feelings in Phoebe's chest grew.

How dare those sparks do this? Looking across at her friends, Phoebe could see they

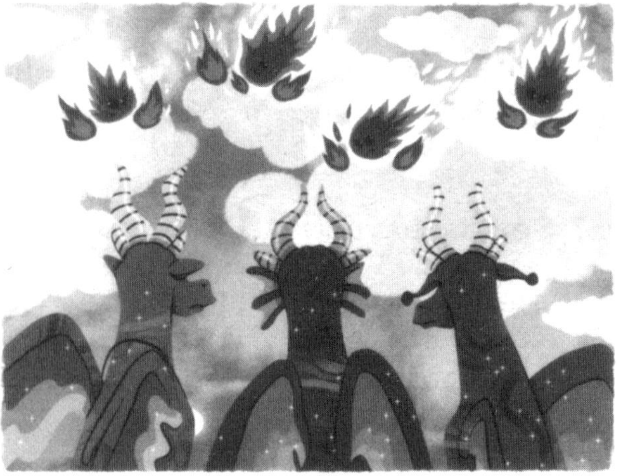

were angry with the Fire Sparks, too. But the angrier they got, the more Fire Sparks appeared. And the brighter and hotter they became!

"We must stay calm," Phoebe called, as much to herself as to the others.

The Fire Sparks rose up in one big, buzzing cloud. They hovered above the Night Dragons.

"I've got a bad feeling about this," muttered Rosie as the Fire Sparks began to dive-bomb them.

The Night Dragons hurried to shield all the Dreamlets from the Fire Sparks with their wings. Luckily their thick scales meant the Dragon Girls did not get hurt, but the attacks weren't fun. More and more Fire Sparks appeared.

"I am really trying not to get mad," Stella said through gritted teeth, "but it's tough. I feel like someone terrible is throwing sparklers at me."

"I know what you mean!" Rosie groaned. "And the Dreamlets look weaker than ever, poor things."

By now, Phoebe was feeling so worked up that it was hard to think straight. *Come on,* she urged herself. *There HAS to be a way to beat the Fire Sparks.* She squeezed her eyes shut for a moment, blocking out all the blazing lights. It was odd how, even though she hated the dark, she often did her best thinking with her eyes closed. It was the opposite of what you'd expect. *The opposite?* Phoebe's mind whirred on that one word, *opposite*.

Opening her eyes, she looked over at her friends. "Instead of trying to squash our anger, let's let it out. In a roar!" she whispered. "We need a roar that's big enough to drown out all these sparks AND cool down the Fire Moon."

Getting really mad was going to be MUCH easier than trying to squish the feelings down! Plus, her mom always told her that was no good anyway.

Stella and Rosie grinned and nodded.

The Fire Sparks seemed to sense that something was up. They were buzzing and attacking the Dragon Girls even more furiously. But that was fine. The madder she and her friends got, the better!

The three Night Dragons breathed in deeply and then roared as one. It felt so good! Phoebe took all her frustration and channeled it into her roar.

Take that, Fire Sparks! she thought triumphantly. *The Night Dragons aren't going to let the bullies win.*

Their mixed roar was incredible. Dazzling moonlight colors billowed up around Phoebe. Her moonlight roar mixed in with the twilight colors of Rosie's roar and the bright starlight of Stella's. There were so many blues and pinks and purples!

Their roar made the clouds tremble. The power of it was too much for the Fire Sparks. The combined roar of the Night Dragons surrounded the sparks, whipping around them like a brightly colored tornado.

When the roar's mist had settled, there wasn't a single Fire Spark to be seen.

The Night Dragons tucked their wings back in and looked down at the little Dreamlets. They were safe!

Weirdly, rather than tiring out Phoebe, roaring had made her feel stronger. She looked over at her friends. Stella and Rosie had stopped roaring and started to laugh and cheer. They looked so happy and relieved, it was impossible for Phoebe not to join in.

The Night Dragons collapsed on the wispy soft clouds. It felt so good to relax. It was like they were at one of their sleepovers, making one another laugh uncontrollably during a pillow fight.

Phoebe sat up and looked around. Something was different. What was it? Then it dawned on her what had changed.

There was no longer an ominous red glow to the moonlight.

"Look!" Rosie cried, also sitting up. "The Fire Moon is gone!"

Phoebe gazed up at the moon. It was once again calm, silver, and beautiful. Exactly how it should be.

The Sky Skimmers had returned and were floating around, beaming. "You did it!" they cried joyfully. "And look how healthy the Dreamlets are now."

It was true. The Dreamlets looked strong and cheery again. With just a few moments in the cool moonlight, they'd become extra fluffy. They leapt through the air in joyful, dreamy arcs.

DasherGirl gave Phoebe a nudge. "It's time to return to the forest," she said. "We need to get these guys back to the Newt Nurses."

Phoebe nodded. "Jump on our backs, every-one! It's time to get you out there, doing your dreamy thing."

With excited squeals, the Dreamlets leapt onto the Night Dragons' backs.

"How do we get down?" Phoebe asked DasherGirl once the little passengers were safely on board.

"You can just swing down on a moonbeam,"

DasherGirl replied, like it was a perfectly normal thing to suggest.

This sounded scarier than being catapulted up here. But now that she had done that and loved it, Phoebe thought that swinging on a moonbeam might be fun after all!

"Can you catch us each a moonbeam, Phoebe?" asked Stella. "They like you the best."

Phoebe scanned the night sky with her powerful moonlight vision. She spotted three perfect moonbeams, moving past like the light of a silver spotlight at a concert. In a flash, she reached out and grabbed all three—one with a front paw, one with a back paw, and one with her tail.

"You really are the Moonlight Dragon!" laughed Rosie as Phoebe handed out the moonbeams.

"And proud of it," Phoebe said, puffing out her blue chest. "Are we ready to soar? Then let's go!"

Together, they bounded over to the edge of the clouds. The Magic Forest stretched out *very* far down below.

"Don't be scared, Dreamlets," Phoebe called to her small charges. "This is going to be fun."

Gripping their moonbeams, Phoebe and her friends leapt off the clouds with a collective *WHOOP.* For a moment, they fell through the air very fast. But then the moonbeams wrapped themselves around the Night Dragons, slowing down the pace of their free fall.

"It feels a bit like we're falling through honey!" Stella called excitedly.

"Yup. Through INVISIBLE honey!" Rosie laughed.

Despite the cool night air, Phoebe felt a warm glow inside. She had never had a dream as wild as THIS!

As they zoomed down toward the Magic Forest, the air became thicker. Soon the Night Dragons were able to use their wings once again.

Phoebe could see the hatchery down below. The Newt Nurses had spotted them and they rushed around excitedly.

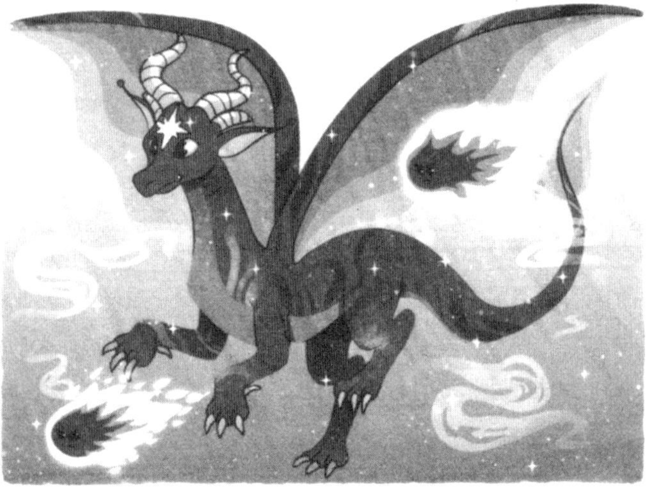

"Ready to land?" Phoebe called.

"You bet!" Rosie called back.

"This is going to be my best landing yet, I can feel it!" Stella yelled.

The hatchery glowed with pearly moonlight as the Dragon Girls landed on the soft grass. Rosie made her usual perfect landing.

Phoebe wobbled a bit but managed to stay upright. Stella did two somersaults, scattering Dreamlets everywhere.

"I totally meant to do that!" Stella declared, laughing as she jumped to her feet. "Are you guys all right?" she asked the Dreamlets. "I hope I didn't squish any of you."

But Stella did not need to worry about the Dreamlets. In fact, they looked like they'd doubled in size since they'd left the clouds. They gathered together in a circle in the center of the hatchery.

A humming noise filled the air, mysterious and beautiful.

"What's going on?" murmured Rosie.

"They are preparing for dream flight," explained a Newt Nurse. "Watch!"

The humming grew louder, and suddenly there was a burst of twinkling light. For a terrible moment, Phoebe thought that the Fire Sparks were back. But this light was soft and cool, nothing like the burning brightness of fire.

The Dreamlets had each grown a pair of wings and were proudly testing them out. The humming sound was still there, but it had changed to something low and gentle. Listening made Phoebe feel happy and sleepy.

"Off you go, darlings!" the Newt Nurses urged

tenderly. "Hum your dreams into the ears of all the sleeping forest creatures."

As a group, the Dreamlets rose up and then floated off in all directions, like seeds from a dandelion blown by the breeze.

Phoebe felt a tug on the magic thread. "We'd better go," Phoebe said, even though she was sad to leave.

DasherGirl nodded. "The Tree Queen is waiting. The thread will lead you back to her glade."

"You're not coming?" Phoebe asked.

The little elk shook her head. "I must leave you. But it was a privilege to share this adventure with you, Moonlight Dragon."

"I loved every moment," said Phoebe. She hated saying goodbye! "Thank you for all your help. I hope we'll get to meet again?"

"I am sure we will," said DasherGirl. And with one last nose rub, the tiny elk rose into the air and darted off between the trees.

Phoebe and her friends spread their wings and flew into the air.

"Thank you, Night Dragons!" called the Newt Nurses as they flew away. "And sweet dreams!"

Phoebe yawned. It had been a long adventure. It must be close to bedtime by now. She gave herself a little shake. She couldn't nod off just yet.

The whole forest felt calm and sleepy in the moonlight. The Night Dragons swooped through the dark sky, and everywhere they looked, they saw daytime creatures yawning as they nestled into their burrows or nests. It was such a relief that the red glow of the Fire Moon was finally gone.

The Tree Queen's glade glowed like a lantern as they drew close. When they pushed through the protective force field, the glade seemed even more magical.

The Tree Queen smiled as they approached. "Well done, Night Dragons! And particularly well done, Phoebe! This was a very difficult quest, but you managed it perfectly."

This made Phoebe feel like she was glowing on the inside.

"Will you call us back again?" asked Rosie in a hopeful voice.

The Tree Queen nodded, her branches swaying. "Yes, and it may be soon. You stopped the Fire Sparks and their queen this time, and we are so grateful. But knowing the Fire Queen, she will gather her strength and return before too long."

"We'd be happy to help," replied Stella, smiling at Phoebe and Rosie. "I think we make a great team."

The Tree Queen nodded in her grand way. "That is definitely true. See you soon, Night

Dragons. And until then, make sure you keep dreaming the biggest dreams you can."

With a swish of her branches, the Tree Queen turned back into a tree.

Phoebe felt a hint of sadness as she and her friends left the glade. But she knew it wouldn't be long before they were back. She yawned again.

"Oh, you're making me yawn!" Rosie said, covering her mouth with a claw. "Rescuing those Dreamlets was tiring, wasn't it?"

"Sure was," said Stella. "Look! There are our bubbles, just like last time. Goodbye for now! You guys are the BEST to go on adventures with."

They gave one another one more wing

hug and then each found their own bubble. Phoebe's was suspended from a branch and had a moonlight glow to it. The closer she got to the bubble, the larger it seemed. Soon it was big enough for her to step inside.

Instantly, a breeze swirled around her, lifting her up and spinning her around before gently placing her down.

When she opened her eyes, Phoebe was back in her bedroom. She was standing by her window, just as she had been before she was called into the forest. She stretched. She was definitely ready for sleep. Climbing into her bed, Phoebe thought about all the adventures she'd just had.

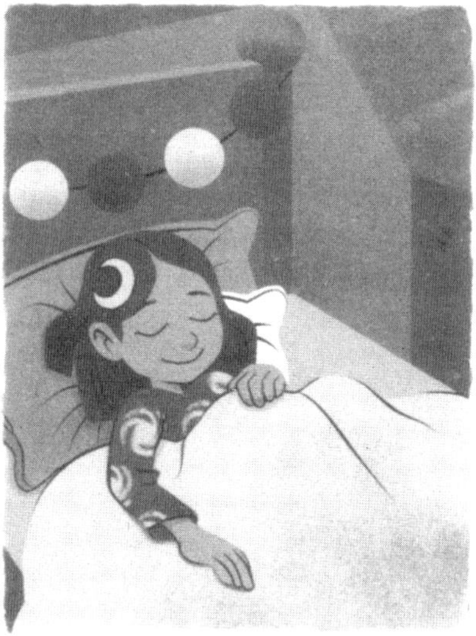

It was like a dream come true. Flying, battling Fire Sparks, meeting funny little creatures. And catching moonbeams up to the clouds! The best part, by far? She and her friends would soon be back in the Magic Forest.

Turn the page for a special sneak peek of Stella's adventure!

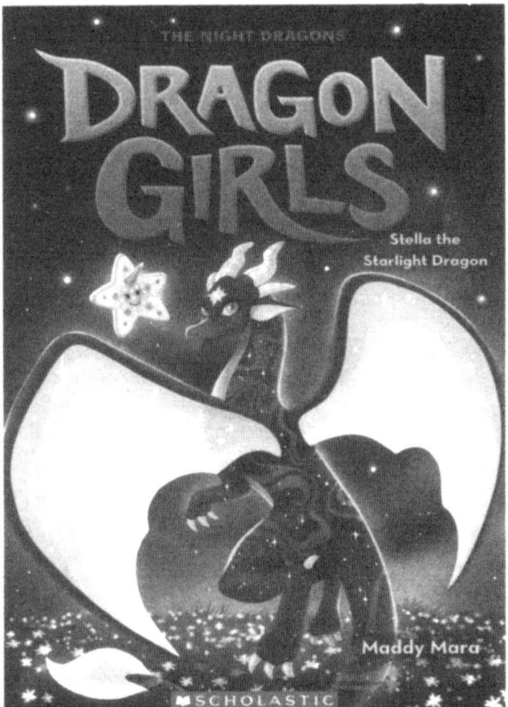

Stella woke to the sound of her alarm. She sat up, feeling confused. Was it time to get up for school? No, it couldn't be. Starlight shone through her bedroom window. Then she saw Rosie and Phoebe, asleep on sleeping bags on the floor. Stella and her two best friends had a sleepover most Friday nights, which meant that it was the weekend.

So why had her alarm gone off? And why was it shoved under her pillow, instead of sitting on her bedside table like usual? Stella quickly turned it off. The clock was shaped like a star. Stella loved anything to do with stars. Her name even *meant* "star"! But that wasn't the only reason she liked stars so much. Ever since she had been very young, Stella had wished on the first star she saw each night. Her favorite wish was always that something magical would happen.

Not so long ago, something *very* magical had happened. And not just to her but to her friends, too. The three girls had been transported into the Magic Forest, where they had become Night Dragons.

Stella was the Starlight Dragon, Rosie was the Twilight Dragon, and Phoebe was the Moonlight Dragon. Stella loved everything about being a dragon. She loved how powerful she felt. She loved roaring whirls of colored smoke that were deliciously and mysteriously cool. She also loved flying, even though she was still learning how to do it the right way.

So far, the Night Dragons had twice been summoned to the Magic Forest. Stella couldn't *wait* until they got called again.

The glowing numbers on her clock read 11:45 p.m. Suddenly, Stella remembered why she had set it in the first place. They were having a midnight feast! She fizzed with excitement as she pushed back the covers and stood up. The sleepover was at her house, so she was in charge of waking the others. Mostly, Sleepover Club was at Phoebe's house because she got homesick the most. But ever since they'd started going to the Magic Forest, Phoebe had become a lot braver. In fact, it had been her suggestion to have tonight's sleepover at Stella's place.

Her friends were still fast asleep as Stella knelt down beside them. "Rosie! Phoebe!" she whispered. "Time to wake up and FEAST!"

Her friends were awake in an instant.

Then Rosie smacked her forehead. "Oops! I left my treats in the kitchen. I'll go and get them now."

"I'll come with you," said Phoebe. "I put some juice in the fridge. Should I get glasses and plates while I'm there?"

"Good idea." Stella nodded. "While you guys do that, I'll set up a comfy spot for us here.

Just be extra quiet so you don't wake my little brother!"

As her friends sneaked out of the room, Stella got busy. She pushed the sleeping bags to one side and grabbed the quilt off her bed. Her grandmother had made it. Little silver and gold stars had been embroidered onto fabric the color of inky-blue sky.

Stella smoothed it out like a picnic blanket on the floor. Then she collected all the pillows and arranged them around the edge. From under her bed she gathered her own offerings for the feast: popcorn and candy. Perfect! Stella stretched out on the quilt to wait for her friends to return.

Stella loved nighttime. She loved the velvety blue-black of the sky, and she loved how quiet it was once the traffic died down and everyone was asleep. You could hear different things at night. Things that were drowned out by the bustle of the day.

In fact, Stella could hear something right now. What was it? She held her breath as a soft, beautiful song floated around her.

Magic Forest, Magic Forest, come explore . . .

The song was familiar. Stella smiled and her heart began to beat faster. This song meant that soon she and her friends would be returning to the forest. From the corner of her eye, Stella saw something strange. One of the stars on her quilt had just moved! She looked at the fabric more closely. An embroidered star shot across the quilt like a comet.

Magic Forest, Magic Forest, come explore . . .

Stella wondered if she should call out to her friends. But as quickly as she had the thought, she dismissed it. They always traveled into the Magic Forest separately.

Anyway, there was no time. The blue of her quilt floated into the air around her. Her bedroom walls began to fade away. A star shot past, sparking as it flew overhead.

Magic Forest, Magic Forest, come explore.

Magic Forest, Magic Forest, hear my roar!

Stella closed her eyes as she whispered the final notes of the enchanted song. Her stomach felt very strange, like she was falling and flying at the same time. But Stella didn't mind one bit. She couldn't wait to return to the Magic Forest!

ABOUT THE AUTHORS

Maddy Mara is the pen name of Australian creative duo Hilary Rogers and Meredith Badger. Hilary and Meredith have been making children's books together for many years. They love dreaming up new ideas and always have lots of projects bubbling away. When not writing, Hilary can be found cooking weird things or going on long walks, often with Meredith. And Meredith can be found teaching English online all around the world or daydreaming about being able to fly. They both currently live in Melbourne, Australia. Their website is maddymara.com.